easy meals

mexican

p

This is a Parragon Publishing Book
This edition published in 2004

Parragon Publishing
Queen Street House
4 Queen Street
Bath BA1 1HE, UK

ISBN: 1-40541-509-6

Printed in China

Produced by The Bridgewater Book Company Ltd, Lewes, East Sussex

Creative Director Terry Jeavons
Art Director Sarah Howerd
Page Make-up Sara Kidd
Editorial Director Fiona Biggs
Senior Editor Mark Truman
Editorial Assistant Tom Kitch

NOTES FOR THE READER

- This book uses both metric and US measurements. Follow the same units of
  measurement throughout; do not mix metric and US measurements.
- All spoon measurements are level: teaspoons are assumed to be 5 ml, and table-
  spoons are assumed to be 15 ml.
- Cup measurements in this book are for American cups.
- Unless otherwise stated, milk is assumed to be whole milk, eggs and individual
  vegetables such as potatoes are medium-sized, and pepper is freshly ground
  black pepper.
- Recipes using raw or very lightly cooked eggs should be avoided by infants, the
  elderly, pregnant women, convalescents, and anyone suffering from an illness.
- Optional ingredients, variations, and serving suggestions have not been included
  in the calculations.
- The times given are an approximate guide only. Preparation times differ according
  to the techniques used by different people and the cooking times vary as a result
  of the type of oven used.

Contents

Introduction

Mexican cooking takes familiar, everyday ingredients—meat and poultry, fish, cheese, and eggs—and presents them in a way that is new and very quick and easy to prepare and cook. The addition of a fiery chile or two, a few garlic cloves, and plenty of fresh cilantro, chopped finely to release its distinctive flavor, transforms a simple dish into a taste sensation, and this is only the beginning. Bell peppers, tomatoes, a whole range of herbs and spices, beans, raisins, and even chocolate find their way into the Mexican cooking pot. Creamy, pale green avocados are a favorite, in salads and as the base of guacamole, a chunky dip. Tortillas, thin, delicious cakes made from maize flour, are as versatile as pasta, rice, or potatoes. They are served with almost everything, in a variety of ways—cut into triangles as an accompaniment or a garnish, or layered with a meat mixture, topped with cheese, and baked, folded, or rolled around a filling.

guide to recipe key	
easy	Recipes are graded as follows: 1 pea = easy; 2 peas = very easy; 3 peas = extremely easy.
serves 4	Recipes generally serve four people. Simply halve the ingredients to serve two, taking care not to mix US and metric measurements.
15 minutes	Preparation time. Where recipes include marinating, soaking, standing, or chilling, these times are listed separately: eg, 15 minutes, plus 30 minutes to marinate.
15 minutes	Cooking time. Cooking times do not include the cooking of accompaniments to be served with the main dishes.

Mexican cooking is great fun for informal meals and for parties. The enticing names of the dishes make a good talking point as they roll lazily off the tongue—pozole, quesadillas, enchiladas, chilaquiles, burritos, fajitas, nachos—and some of the recipes can even be assembled by guests, because to serve a pot of sizzling hot spicy meat, a plate of crisp raw vegetables, some cool sour cream, and a stack of warm tortillas, and invite them to create their own dish, is a wonderful ice-breaker. Add one or two colorful salsas, be prepared to shed your inhibitions about food and eating when you experiment with Mexican cooking.

Classic Beef Fajitas, page 36

Soups & Appetizers

Mexican soups and appetizers can make a stylish start to a meal. If you think of soups as light and bland, the Yucatecan Citrus Soup, combining the kick of garlic and chiles with the refreshing zing of citrus zest and juice, you may change your mind. The tangy flavor of Authentic Guacamole will challenge your preconceptions, as well as your taste buds, and for an appetizer to linger and chat over, serve Chorizo Artichoke Heart Quesadillas, a heart-warming dish of warm tortillas topped with meat and melting, bubbling cheese. And for hot days there is Iced Salsa Soup.

Mexican-Style Beef & Rice Soup

3 tbsp olive oil
1 lb 2 oz/500 g boneless
   stewing beef, cut into
   1 inch/2.5 cm pieces
²⁄₃ cup red wine
1 onion, chopped finely
1 green bell pepper,
   cored, deseeded, and
   chopped finely
1 small fresh red chile,
   deseeded and
   chopped finely
2 garlic cloves, chopped
   finely
1 carrot, chopped finely
¼ tsp ground coriander
¼ tsp ground cumin
⅛ tsp ground cinnamon
¼ tsp dried oregano
1 bay leaf
grated zest of ½ orange
14 oz/400 g canned
   chopped tomatoes
5 cups beef bouillon
¼ cup long-grain white
   rice
3 tbsp raisins
½ oz/15 g semisweet
   chocolate, melted
chopped fresh cilantro,
   to garnish

❶ Heat half the oil in a large skillet over a medium—high heat. Add the meat in one layer and cook until well browned, turning to color all sides. Remove the pan from the heat and pour in the wine.

❷ Heat the remaining oil in a large pan over a medium heat. Add the onion, then cover, and cook for about 3 minutes, stirring occasionally, until just softened. Add the green bell pepper, chile, garlic, and carrot, and continue cooking, covered, for 3 minutes.

❸ Add the coriander, cumin, cinnamon, oregano, bay leaf, and orange zest. Stir in the tomatoes and bouillon with the beef and wine. Bring almost to a boil, and when the mixture begins to bubble, reduce the heat to low. Cover, and simmer gently, stirring occasionally, for about 1 hour, or until the meat is tender.

❹ Stir in the rice, raisins, and chocolate, and continue cooking, stirring occasionally, for about 30 minutes, or until the rice is tender.

❺ Ladle into warm bowls and garnish with cilantro.

very easy

serves 4

15 minutes

2 hours

Piquant Oatmeal Soup

INGREDIENTS

1 cup rolled oatmeal
3 tbsp butter
1 large sweet onion,
    chopped finely
2–3 garlic cloves
12 oz/350 g tomatoes,
    skinned, deseeded,
    and chopped
6 cups chicken bouillon
⅛ tsp ground cumin
1 tsp harissa, or ½ tsp
    chili paste
1–2 tbsp lime juice
salt and pepper
chopped scallions, to
    garnish

 very easy

 serves 4

 10 minutes

 45 minutes

❶ Place a heavy-based skillet over a medium heat. Add the oatmeal and toast for about 25 minutes, stirring frequently, until lightly and evenly browned. Remove the oats from the pan and let cool.

❷ Heat the butter in a large pan over a medium heat. Add the onion and garlic, and cook until the onion is softened.

❸ Add the tomatoes, bouillon, cumin, and the harissa or chili paste, plus a good pinch of salt to the softened onion and garlic.

❹ Stir in the toasted oatmeal and bring to a boil. Regulate the heat so the soup boils gently and cook for 6 minutes.

❺ Stir in 1 tablespoon of the lime juice. Taste and adjust the seasoning. Add more lime juice if desired. Ladle the soup into warm bowls, and serve sprinkled with scallions, to garnish.

Iced Salsa Soup

INGREDIENTS

2 large ears of corn, or
  8 oz/225 g. frozen
  corn kernels
1 tbsp olive oil
1 orange or red bell
  pepper, cored,
  deseeded, and
  chopped finely
1 green bell pepper,
  cored, deseeded, and
  chopped finely
1 sweet onion, such as
  Vidalia, chopped
  finely
3 ripe tomatoes,
  skinned, deseeded,
  and chopped
½ tsp chili powder, or to
  taste
½ cup water
2 cups tomato juice
chili paste (optional)
salt and pepper

TO GARNISH
3–4 scallions, chopped
  finely
cilantro

❶ Cut the corn kernels from the cobs, or defrost and drain the frozen corn kernels.

❷ Heat the oil in a pan over a medium–high heat. Add the bell peppers and cook, stirring briskly, for 3 minutes. Add the onion and continue cooking for about 2 minutes, or until it starts to color slightly.

❸ Add the tomatoes, corn, and chili powder. Continue cooking, stirring frequently, for 1 minute. Pour in the water and when it bubbles, reduce the heat, cover, and cook for an additional 4–5 minutes, or until the bell peppers are just barely tender.

❹ Transfer the mixture to a large container and stir in the tomato juice. Season with salt and pepper, and add more chili powder if desired. Cover, and refrigerate until cold.

❺ Taste and adjust the seasoning. For a more spicy soup, stir in a little chili paste to taste. For a thinner soup, add a small amount of iced water. Ladle into chilled bowls and garnish with scallions and cilantro.

very easy

serves 4

15 minutes, plus
4 hours to chill

15 minutes

Yucatecan Citrus Soup

INGREDIENTS

2 onions
15 large garlic cloves,
    unpeeled
1 tbsp olive oil
6 cups vegetable,
    chicken, or fish
    bouillon
1 cup water
8 ripe tomatoes, diced
pinch of dried oregano
1 green chile, such as
    jalapeño or serrano,
    deseeded and
    chopped
pinch of ground cumin
$\frac{1}{2}$ tsp finely grated
    grapefruit zest
$\frac{1}{2}$ tsp finely grated lime
    zest
$\frac{1}{2}$ tsp finely grated
    orange zest
juice and diced flesh of
    2 limes
juice of 1 orange
juice of 1 grapefruit
salt and pepper

TO GARNISH
tortilla chips, or sliced
    tortilla strips fried
    until crisp
2 tbsp chopped fresh
    cilantro

 easy

serves 4–6

15 minutes

1 hour

❶ Cut one onion in half without peeling. Peel the second onion and chop it finely.

❷ Heat a large heavy-based skillet, add the unpeeled onion halves and the garlic, and cook over a medium–high heat until the skins char and the onions are caramelized on their cut sides; the garlic should be soft on the inside. Remove the onion and garlic from the pan and let stand until cool enough to handle.

❸ Meanwhile, heat the oil in a pan and lightly sauté the remaining onion until it is softened. Add the bouillon and water, and bring to a boil. Reduce the heat and simmer for a few minutes.

❹ Peel the charred onion and garlic, then chop coarsely and add to the simmering soup with the tomatoes, chile, oregano, and cumin. Cook for about 15 minutes, stirring occasionally.

❺ Add the citrus zest, season with salt and pepper, then simmer for another 2 minutes. Remove from the heat and stir in the lime flesh and citrus juices.

❻ Ladle into soup bowls, garnish with tortilla chips and fresh cilantro, and serve immediately.

Pozole

❶ Place the pork and chicken in a large pan. Add enough water to fill the pan. (Do not worry about making too much bouillon. It has many uses, keeps fresh for up to a week, and freezes well.)

❷ Bring to a boil, then skim off the fat that rises to the surface. Reduce the heat and add the bouillon cube, garlic, onion, and bay leaves. Simmer, covered, over a medium–low heat until the pork and chicken are tender and cooked through.

❸ Remove the pork and chicken from the soup and let cool. When cool enough to handle, remove the chicken flesh from the bones and cut the pork into bite-sized pieces. Set aside for later use.

❹ Skim the fat off the soup and discard the bay leaves. Add the hominy, cumin, salt, and pepper to taste. Bring to a boil.

❺ To serve, place a little pork and chicken in soup bowls. Top with cabbage, oregano, and chili flakes, then spoon in the hot soup. Serve with tortilla chips and lime.

❸ 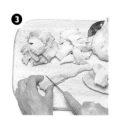 ❹  ❺

 very easy

 serves 4–6

 15 minutes

1 hour

Authentic Guacamole

INGREDIENTS

1 ripe tomato
2 limes
2–3 ripe small–medium
    avocados, or 1–2
    large ones
$\frac{1}{4}$–$\frac{1}{2}$ onion, chopped
    finely
pinch of ground cumin
pinch of mild chili
    powder
$\frac{1}{2}$–1 fresh green chiles,
    such as jalapeño or
    serrano, deseeded
    and chopped finely
1 tbsp chopped finely
    fresh cilantro leaves,
    plus extra for
    garnishing
salt (optional)
tortilla chips, to serve
    (optional)

 extremely easy

 serves 4–6

 10 minutes

0 minutes

❶ To skin the tomato, place in a heatproof bowl, then pour boiling water over to cover it, and let stand for 30 seconds. Drain and plunge into cold water. The skins will then slide off easily. Cut in half, deseed, and chop the flesh.

❷ Squeeze the juice from the limes into a bowl. Cut each avocado in half around the pit. Twist apart, then remove the pit with a knife. Peel off the skin carefully, then dice the flesh and toss it in the bowl of lime juice to prevent discoloration. Repeat with the remaining avocados. Mash the avocados coarsely.

❸ Add the onion, tomato, cumin, chili powder, chiles, and fresh cilantro to the avocados. If using as a dip for tortilla chips, do not add salt. If using as a sauce, add salt to taste.

❹ To serve as a dip, transfer to a serving dish, then garnish with cilantro and serve with tortilla chips.

COOK'S TIP

Avocados grow in abundance in Mexico, and Guacamole is used to add richness and flavor to many dishes. It is spooned into soups and spread on tortas (thick, crusty rolls).

Salpicón of Crab

INGREDIENTS

$\frac{1}{4}$ red onion, chopped
$\frac{1}{2}$–1 green chile,
   deseeded and
   chopped
juice of $\frac{1}{2}$ lime
1 tbsp cider vinegar or
   other fruit vinegar,
   such as raspberry
1 tbsp chopped fresh
   cilantro
1 tbsp extra-virgin
   olive oil
8–12 oz/225–350 g fresh
   crab meat
lettuce leave, to serve

GARNISH
1 avocado
lime juice, for tossing
1–2 ripe tomatoes
3–5 radishes

extremely easy

serves 4

15 minutes

0 minutes

❶ Combine the onion with the chile, lime juice, vinegar, fresh cilantro, and olive oil. Add the crab meat and toss the ingredients lightly.

❷ To make the garnish, cut each avocado in half around the pit. Twist apart, then remove the pit with a knife. Carefully peel off the skin and slice the flesh. Toss gently in lime juice to prevent discoloration.

❸ Halve the tomatoes, then remove the cores and seeds. Dice the flesh. Slice the radishes thinly.

❹ Arrange the crab salad on a bed of lettuce leaves, then garnish with the avocado, tomatoes, and radishes. Serve at once.

VARIATION
Split open a long roll or a baguette, and heap salpicón salad inside. Top with a generous layer of cheese, then place the open roll under the grill and toast to melt the cheese. Serve with salsa.

Chorizo & Artichoke Heart Quesadillas

❶ Dice the chorizo sausage. Heat a heavy-based skillet, then add the chorizo and cook until it browns in places.

❷ If using the mild chile or bell pepper, place under a preheated hot broiler and broil for about 10 minutes, or until the skins are charred and the flesh softened. Place in a plastic bag and twist to seal, then set aside for 20 minutes. Remove the skins with a knife, then deseed and chop.

❸ Arrange the browned chorizo and artichoke hearts on the corn tortillas, then transfer half to a baking sheet.

❹ Sprinkle with the garlic, then the cheese. Place under a preheated hot broiler and broil until the cheese melts and sizzles. Repeat with the remaining tortillas.

❺ Sprinkle with the diced tomato, scallions, green chile or bell pepper (if using), and fresh cilantro. Cut into wedges and serve.

 very easy

serves 4

 10 minutes, plus 20 minutes standing time

10 minutes

Meat

Mexican meat dishes are robust, rich, and comforting. Many combine beef, pork, lamb, chicken, or sausage with beans and a generous quantity of cheese. For a lighter variation on this theme, try the Steak, Avocado, & Bean Salad with a mildly spiced lime and olive oil dressing, garnished with crisp tortilla chips. Meatballs in Spicy-Sweet Sauce transforms meat by cooking it with colorful diced sweet potatoes, and serving it with grated cheese. Santa Fe Red Chili Enchiladas uses tortillas imaginatively by stacking them in layers, interspersed with a filling of chili paste and chicken, and topped with a fried egg.

Steak, Avocado, & Bean Salad

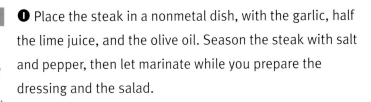

INGREDIENTS

12 oz/350 g tender
  steak, such as sirloin
4 garlic cloves, chopped
juice of 1 lime
4 tbsp extra-virgin olive oil
1 tbsp white or red wine
  vinegar
¼ tsp mild chili powder
¼ tsp ground cumin
½ tsp paprika
pinch of sugar (optional)
5 scallions, sliced thinly
about 7 oz/200 g crisp
  lettuce leaves, such
  as romaine
14 oz/400 g canned
  pinto, black, or red
  kidney beans
1 avocado, pitted,
  sliced, and tossed
  with a little lime juice
2 ripe tomatoes, diced
¼ green or red chile,
  chopped
3 tbsp chopped fresh
  cilantro
8 oz/225 g canned corn,
  drained
generous handful of
  crisp tortilla chips,
  broken into pieces
salt and pepper

❶ Place the steak in a nonmetal dish, with the garlic, half the lime juice, and the olive oil. Season the steak with salt and pepper, then let marinate while you prepare the dressing and the salad.

❷ To make the dressing, combine the remaining lime juice and olive oil with the vinegar, chili powder, cumin, and paprika. Add a pinch of sugar to taste. Set aside.

❸ Pan-fry the steak, or cook under a preheated broiler, until browned on the outside and cooked to your liking in the middle. Remove from the pan, cut into strips and reserve, keeping warm or letting cool.

❹ Toss the scallions with the lettuce and arrange on a serving plate. Pour about half the dressing over the leaves, then arrange the beans, avocado, and tomatoes over the top. Sprinkle with the chile, cilantro, and corn.

❺ Arrange the steak and the tortilla chips on top, then pour the rest of the dressing over them. Serve immediately.

 very easy

 serves 4

 10 minutes

 5–10 minutes

Santa Fe Red Chili Enchiladas

INGREDIENTS

2-3 tbsp masa harina, or
   1 corn tortilla,
   crushed or crumbled
4 tbsp mild chili powder,
   such as New Mexico
2 tbsp paprika
2 garlic cloves, chopped
   finely
¼ tsp ground cumin
pinch of ground
   cinnamon
pinch of ground allspice
pinch of dried oregano
4 cups vegetable,
   chicken, or beef
   bouillon, simmering
1 tbsp lime juice
1–2 tbsp extra-virgin
   olive oil
12 flour tortillas
about 1 lb/450 g cooked
   chicken or pork, cut
   into pieces
¾ cup grated cheese
4–6 eggs

TO SERVE
½ onion, chopped finely
1 tbsp finely chopped
   fresh cilantro
salsa of your choice

❶ Mix the masa harina with the chili powder, paprika, garlic, cumin, cinnamon, allspice, oregano, and enough water to make a thin paste. Process in a blender or a food processor until smooth.

❷ Stir the paste into the simmering bouillon, then reduce the heat and cook until it thickens slightly. Remove the sauce from the heat and stir in the lime juice.

❸ Dip the tortillas into the warm sauce. Cover one tortilla with cooked meat. Top with a second dipped tortilla and more meat, making a stack. Make 1–2 more stacks in this way, then transfer them to an ovenproof dish.

❹ Pour the remaining sauce over the tortillas, then sprinkle the grated cheese over the top. Bake the tortillas in a preheated oven at 350°F/180°C for 15–20 minutes, or until the cheese has melted.

❺ Meanwhile, heat the olive oil in a nonstick skillet and cook the eggs until the whites are set, but the yolks still soft.

❻ Cut into wedges and serve topped with an egg and garnished with the onion, cilantro, and salsa.

 very easy

 serves 4–6

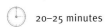 10 minutes

20–25 minutes

Casserole of Tortilla Chips & Chorizo

INGREDIENTS

12 stale tortillas, cut
    into strips
1 tbsp vegetable oil
2–3 chorizo sausages,
    sliced thinly or diced
2 garlic cloves, chopped
    finely
8 oz/225 g chopped
    canned tomatoes
3 tbsp chopped fresh
    cilantro
2 cups chicken or
    vegetable bouillon
2 cups grated cheese
1 onion, chopped finely
salt and pepper

❶ Place the tortilla strips in a roasting pan and toss with the oil, then bake in a preheated oven at 375°F/190 °C for about 30 minutes, or until they are crisp and golden.

❷ Brown the chorizo with the garlic in a skillet until the meat is cooked. Pour away any excess fat. Add the tomatoes and the cilantro to the pan, and season with salt and pepper to taste. Set aside.

❸ In an ovenproof dish about 12 inches/30 cm square, layer the tortilla chips and chorizo mixture, finishing with the tortilla chips.

❹ Pour the bouillon over the top of the dish, then sprinkle with the cheese. Bake in a preheated oven at 375° F/190° C for about 40 minutes, or until the cheese has melted and the tortilla chips are fairly soft.

❺ Serve immediately, sprinkled with the chopped onion.

 extremely easy

 serves 4

 10 minutes

 1 hour,
20 minutes

Green Chili and Chicken Chilaquiles

*12 stale tortillas, cut
   into strips
1 tbsp vegetable oil
1 small cooked chicken,
   meat removed from
   the bones and cut
   into bite-sized pieces
salsa verde
8 tbsp chopped fresh
   cilantro
1 tsp finely chopped
   fresh oregano
   or thyme
4 garlic cloves, chopped
   finely
1/4 tsp ground cumin
3 cups grated cheese,
   such as Cheddar,
   Manchego, or
   mozzarella
2 cups chicken bouillon
about 1 1/3 cups freshly
   grated Parmesan
   cheese*

TO SERVE
*1 1/2 cups crème fraîche
   or sour cream
3–5 scallions, sliced
   thinly
pickled chilis*

❶ Place the tortilla strips in a roasting pan and toss with the oil, then bake in a preheated oven at 375° F/190° C for about 30 minutes, or until they are crisp and golden.

❷ Arrange the chicken in a 9 x 13 inch/23 x 33 cm casserole, then sprinkle with half the salsa verde, cilantro, oregano, garlic, cumin, and cheese. Repeat these layers and top with the tortilla strips.

❸ Pour the bouillon over the top, then sprinkle with the remaining cheeses.

❹ Bake in a preheated oven at 375° F/190 ° C for about 30 minutes, or until the cheese is lightly golden in areas.

❺ Garnish with the crème fraîche, scallions, and pickled chilis. Serve at once.

 extremely easy

 serves 4

 15 minutes

 1 hour

Burritos of Lamb & Black Beans

INGREDIENTS

1 lb 5 oz/600 g lean
    lamb
3 garlic cloves, chopped
    finely
juice of ½ a lime
½ tsp mild chili powder
½ tsp ground cumin
large pinch of dried
    oregano leaves,
    crushed
1–2 tbsp extra-virgin
    olive oil
14 oz/400 g cooked
    black beans,
    seasoned with a little
    cumin, salt, and
    pepper
4 large flour tortillas
2–3 tbsp chopped fresh
    cilantro
salsa, preferably a
    chipotle salsa
salt and pepper

❶ Slice the lamb into thin strips, then combine with the garlic, lime juice, chili powder, cumin, oregano, and olive oil. Season with salt and pepper. Marinate in the refrigerator for 4 hours.

❷ Warm the black beans with a little water in a pan.

❸ Heat the tortillas in an ungreased nonstick skillet, sprinkling them with a few drops of water as they heat. Wrap the tortillas in a clean dish towel as you work to keep them warm. Alternatively, heat through in a stack in the pan, alternating the top and bottom tortillas so that they warm evenly, and wrap them to keep them warm.

❹ Stir-fry the lamb in a heavy-based nonstick skillet over high heat until it is browned on all sides. Remove the meat from the heat.

❺ Spoon some of the beans and browned meat into a tortilla, sprinkle with cilantro, then dab with salsa and roll up. Repeat with the remaining tortillas and serve at once.

extremely easy

serves 4

15 minutes, plus
4 hours to
marinate

20 minutes

Classic Beef Fajitas

INGREDIENTS

1 lb 9 oz/700 g beef skirt
    steak or other tender
    steak, cut into strips
6 garlic cloves, chopped
juice of 1 lime
large pinch of mild chili
    powder
large pinch of paprika
large pinch of ground
    cumin
1–2 tbsp extra-virgin
    olive oil
12 flour tortillas
vegetable oil
1–2 avocados, pitted,
    sliced, and tossed
    with lime juice
½ cup sour cream
salt and pepper

PICO DE GALLO SALSA
8 ripe tomatoes, diced
3 scallions, thinly sliced
1–2 green chiles, such
    as jalapeño or
    serrano, deseeded
    and chopped
3–4 tbsp chopped fresh
    cilantro
5–8 radishes, diced
ground cumin

❶ Combine the beef with half the garlic, half the lime juice, the chili powder, paprika, cumin, and olive oil. Add salt and pepper, mix well, and let marinate for at least 30 minutes at room temperature, or, preferably, overnight in the refrigerator.

❷ To make the pico de gallo salsa, put the tomatoes in a bowl with the scallions, green chile, cilantro, and radishes. Season to taste with cumin, salt, and pepper. Set aside.

❸ Heat the tortillas in a lightly greased nonstick frying pan; wrap in aluminum foil as you work, to keep them warm.

❹ Stir-fry the meat in a little oil over a high heat until browned and just cooked through.

❺ Serve the sizzling hot meat with the warm tortillas, the pico de gallo salsa, the avocado, and the sour cream for each person to make his or her own rolled-up fajitas.

 extremely easy

 serves 4–6

 20 minutes,
30 minutes to
marinate

 10–15 minutes

Michoacan Beef

INGREDIENTS

about 3 tbsp all-
   purpose flour
2 lb 4 oz/1 kg stewing
   beef, cut into bite-
   sized pieces
2 tbsp vegetable oil
2 onions, chopped
5 garlic cloves, chopped
14 oz/400 g tomatoes,
   diced
1½ dried chipotle chilis,
   reconstituted,
   deseeded, and cut
   into thin strips, or a
   few shakes of bottled
   chipotle salsa
6¼ cups beef bouillon
12 oz/350 g green beans,
   trimmed
a pinch of sugar
salt and pepper

TO SERVE
simmered beans
cooked rice

❶ Place the flour in a large bowl and season with salt and pepper. Add the beef and toss to coat well. Remove from the bowl, shaking off the excess flour.

❷ Heat the oil in a skillet and brown the meat briefly over a high heat. Reduce the heat to medium, then add the onions and garlic, and cook for another 2 minutes.

❸ Add the tomatoes, chilis, and bouillon, then cover and simmer over a low heat for 1½ hours, or until the meat is very tender, adding the green beans 15 minutes before the end of the cooking time. Skim off any fat that rises to the surface.

❹ Transfer to individual bowls and serve with the simmered beans and cooked rice.

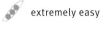 extremely easy

 serves 4

 15 minutes

 1 hour,
40 minutes

Meatballs in Spicy-Sweet Sauce

INGREDIENTS

8 oz/225 g ground pork
8 oz/225 g ground beef
   or lamb
6 tbsp cooked rice or finely
   crushed tortilla chips
1 egg, beaten lightly
1½ onions, chopped
5 garlic cloves, chopped
   finely
½ tsp ground cumin
large pinch of ground
   cinnamon
2 tbsp raisins
1 tbsp dark brown sugar
1–2 tbsp cider vinegar,
   or wine vinegar
14 oz/400 g canned
   tomatoes, drained
   and chopped
1¼ cups beef bouillon
1–2 tbsp mild chili
   powder
1 tbsp paprika
1 tbsp chopped fresh
   cilantro
1 tbsp chopped fresh
   parsley or mint
2 tbsp vegetable oil
2 sweet potatoes,
   peeled and cut into
   bite-sized pieces
salt and pepper
grated cheese, to serve

❶ Mix the meat with the rice or crushed tortilla chips, the egg, half the onion, half the garlic, the cumin, cinnamon, and raisins.

❷ Divide the mixture into even-sized pieces and roll into balls. Fry the balls in a nonstick skillet over a medium heat, adding a drop or two of oil, if necessary, to help them brown. Remove from the pan and set aside.

❸ Place the brown sugar in a blender or a food processor, with the vinegar, tomatoes, bouillon, chili powder, paprika, and remaining onion and garlic. Process, then stir in the chopped fresh herbs. Set aside.

❹ Heat the oil in the cleaned skillet, then add the sweet potatoes and cook them until they are tender and golden. Pour in the blended sauce and add the meatballs. Cook for about 10 minutes, or until the meatballs are heated through and the flavors have combined. Season with salt and pepper to taste. Serve accompanied by grated cheese.

very easy

serves 4

15 minutes

45 minutes

Spicy Meat & Chipotle Hash

1 onion, chopped finely
1 tbsp vegetable oil
1 lb/450 g leftover meat,
     such as simmered
     pork or beef, cooled
     and cut into strips
1 tbsp mild chili powder
2 ripe tomatoes,
     deseeded and diced
about 1 cup meat bouillon
½–1 canned chipotle
     chilis, mashed, plus a
     little of the marinade,
     or a few shakes
     bottled chipotle salsa
½ cup sour cream
4–6 tbsp chopped fresh
     cilantro
4–6 tbsp chopped radishes
3–4 leaves crisp lettuce,
     such as romaine,
     shredded
flour tortillas, to serve

 very easy

 serves 4

 10 minutes

30 minutes

❶ Heat the oil in a skillet, then add the onion and cook until softened, stirring occasionally. Add the meat and sauté for about 3 minutes, stirring, until lightly browned.

❷ Add the chili powder, tomatoes, and bouillon and cook until the tomatoes reduce to a sauce, mashing the meat a little as it cooks.

❸ Add the chipotle chilis and continue to cook and mash until the sauce and meat are almost blended.

❹ Serve the dish with a stack of warmed corn tortillas for guests to fill with the meaty mixture to make tacos. Also serve sour cream, fresh cilantro, radishes, and lettuce to add to the meat.

COOK'S TIP
Serve with 2 sliced avocados, tossed with lime juice. Their bland taste and smooth texture make an interesting contrast to the spicy meat.

Fish

Many Mexican fish recipes include chiles, garlic, and cilantro—their taste usually complemented with the juice of a lime. Several dishes in this section are based on this delicious combination of flavors, all very quick and easy—Pan-Fried Scallops Mexicana can be prepared and cooked in moments. By contrast, Squid simmered with Tomatoes, Olives, & Capers is cooked with additional herbs and spices to a stewlike consistency. Fish with Yucatecan flavors is a dish from the Yucatan. The fish is dressed with a paste of fruit juice mixed with spices, wrapped in banana leaves, and steamed.

Fish with Yucatecan flavors

INGREDIENTS

4 tbsp annatto seeds,
    soaked in water
    overnight
3 garlic cloves, chopped
    finely
1 tbsp mild chili powder
1 tbsp paprika
1 tsp ground cumin
½ tsp dried oregano
2 tbsp beer or tequila
juice of 1 lime and
    1 orange or 3 tbsp
    pineapple juice
2 tbsp olive oil
2 tbsp chopped fresh
    cilantro
¼ tsp ground cinnamon
¼ tsp ground cloves
2 lb 4 oz/1 kg swordfish
    steaks
banana leaves, for
    wrapping (optional)
fresh cilantro leaves, to
    garnish
orange wedges, to
    serve

❶ Drain the annatto seeds, put them in a mortar, and crush them to a paste with a pestle. Work in the garlic, chili powder, paprika, cumin, oregano, beer or tequila, fruit juice, olive oil, fresh cilantro, cinnamon, and cloves.

❷ Smear the paste onto the fish and marinate in the refrigerator for at least 3 hours or overnight.

❸ Wrap the fish steak in banana leaves, tying with string to make packages. Bring water to a boil in a steamer, then add the packages to the top part of the steamer and cook for about 15 minutes, or until the fish is cooked through.

❹ Alternatively, cook the fish without wrapping it in the banana leaves. To cook on the barbecue grill, enclose it in a hinged basket, or place it on a rack, and cook over the hot coals for 5–6 minutes on each side, or until cooked through. Or cook the fish under a preheated broiler for 5–6 minutes on each side, or until cooked through.

❺ Garnish with cilantro and serve with orange wedges for squeezing over the fish.

 easy

 serves 4

 20 minutes, plus 3 hours to marinate

20–25 minutes

Shrimp in Green Bean Sauce

INGREDIENTS

3 onions, chopped
5 garlic cloves, chopped
2 tbsp vegetable oil
5–7 ripe tomatoes,
 diced
6–8 oz/175–225 g green
 beans, cut into 2 inch
 /5 cm pieces and
 blanched in boiling
 water for 1 minute
¼ tsp ground cumin
pinch of ground allspice
pinch of ground
 cinnamon
½–1 canned chipotle
 chili in adobo mari-
 nade, with some of
 the marinade
2 cups fish bouillon or
 water mixed with a
 fish bouillon cube
1 lb raw shrimp, peeled
fresh cilantro sprigs
1 lime, cut into wedges

❶ Fry the onion and garlic lightly in the oil over a low heat for 5–10 minutes, or until softened. Add the tomatoes and cook for an additional 2 minutes.

❷ Add the green beans, cumin, allspice, cinnamon, the chipotle chili and adobe marinade, and the fish bouillon. Bring to a boil, then reduce the heat and simmer for a few minutes to combine the flavors.

❸ Add the shrimp and cook for 1–2 minutes only, then remove the pan from the heat and let the shrimp steep in the hot liquid to finish cooking. They are cooked when they have turned bright pink.

❹ Serve immediately, garnished with the fresh cilantro and accompanied by the lime wedges.

 very easy

 serves 4

 10 minutes

 25 minutes

Squid simmered with Tomatoes, Olives & Capers

❶ Heat the oil in a pan and fry the squid lightly until it turns opaque. Season with salt and pepper, and remove from the pan with a slotted spoon.

❷ Add the onion and garlic to the remaining oil in the pan and fry until softened. Stir in the tomatoes, chiles, herbs, cinnamon, allspice, sugar, and olives. Cover and cook over a medium–low heat for 5–10 minutes, or until the mixture thickens slightly. Uncover the pan and cook for an additional 5 minutes to concentrate the flavors.

❸ Stir in the reserved squid and any of the juices that have gathered. Add the capers and heat through.

❹ Adjust the seasoning, then serve immediately, garnished with fresh cilantro.

 very easy

 serves 4–6

 10 minutes

30 minutes

Pan-Fried Scallops Mexicana

2 tbsp butter
2 tbsp extra-virgin olive
oil
1 lb 6 oz/625 g scallops,
shelled
4–5 scallions, sliced
thinly
3–4 garlic cloves,
chopped finely
½ green chile, deseeded
and chopped finely
2 tbsp finely chopped
fresh cilantro
juice of ½ lime
salt and pepper
lime wedges, to serve

❶ Heat half the butter and olive oil in a heavy-based skillet until the butter foams, then add the scallops and cook quickly until they just turn opaque. Do not overcook. Remove from the pan with a slotted spoon and keep warm.

❷ Add the remaining butter and oil to the pan, then toss in the scallions and garlic and cook over a medium heat until the scallions wilt. Return the scallops to the pan.

❸ Remove the pan from the heat and add the chile, cilantro, and lime juice. Season with salt and pepper and stir to mix well.

❹ Serve immediately with lime wedges to squeeze over the scallops.

 extremely easy

 serves 4

 10 minutes

 10 minutes

Spicy Broiled Salmon

4 salmon steaks, 6–8 oz/
175–225 g each
lime slices, to garnish

MARINADE
4 garlic cloves, chopped
finely
2 tbsp extra-virgin olive oil
pinch of ground allspice
pinch ground cinnamon
juice of 2 limes
1–2 tsp marinade from
canned or bottled
chipotle chilis, or chili
salsa
$\frac{1}{4}$ tsp ground cumin
pinch of sugar
salt and pepper

TO SERVE
tomato wedges
3 scallions, chopped
shredded lettuce

❶ To make the marinade, chop the garlic finely, and place it in a bowl with the olive oil, allspice, cinnamon, lime juice, chipotle marinade, cumin, and sugar. Add salt and pepper, and stir to combine.

❷ Coat the salmon with the garlic mixture, then place in a nonmetal dish. Let marinate for at least an hour, or preferably overnight in the refrigerator.

❸ Transfer to a broiler pan and cook under a preheated broiler for 3–4 minutes on each side. Alternatively, cook the salmon over hot coals on a grill until cooked through.

❹ To serve, mix the tomato wedges with the scallions. Place the salmon on individual plates and arrange the tomato salad and shredded lettuce alongside. Garnish with lime slices, and serve.

extremely easy

serves 4

10 minutes,
plus 1–8 hours
to marinate

8 minutes

Fish Baked with Lime

INGREDIENTS

2 lb 4 oz/1 kg white fish
   fillets, such as bass,
   flounder, or cod
1 lime, halved
3 tbsp extra-virgin olive
   oil
1 large onion, chopped
   finely
3 garlic cloves, chopped
   finely
2–3 pickled jalapeño
   chilis (see Cook's
   Tip), chopped
6–8 tbsp chopped fresh
   cilantro
salt and pepper
lemon and lime wedges,
   to serve

❶ Place the fish fillets in a bowl and sprinkle with salt and pepper. Squeeze the juice from the lime over the fish.

❷ Heat the olive oil in a skillet. Add the onion and garlic and fry for about 2 minutes, stirring frequently, until softened. Remove from the heat.

❸ Place one-third of the onion mixture and a little of the chili and cilantro in the bottom of a shallow baking dish or roasting pan. Arrange the fish on top. Sprinkle with the remaining onion mixture, chili, and cilantro.

❹ Bake in a preheated oven at 350°F/180°C for 15–20 minutes, or until the fish has become slightly opaque and firm to the touch. Serve at once, with lemon and lime wedges for squeezing over the fish.

extremely easy

serves 4

10 minutes

25 minutes

COOK'S TIP
Pickled jalapeños are called jalapeños en escabeche and are available from specialty stores.

Salads, Snacks & Side Dishes

Many Mexican snack dishes are based on refried beans. These are pinto beans which are cooked and mashed, then refried with seasonings and onions. The classic recipe, on page 62, is aptly named Mexican Refried Beans "with everything." No Mexican feast would be complete without salsas and sauces (or *moles*) to accompany the beans, and these pages include recipes for Hot Mexican Salsas and Mole Poblano, which includes chocolate among its mix of ingredients.

Hot Mexican Salsas

INGREDIENTS

TROPICAL FRUIT SALSA
½ sweet ripe pineapple,
  peeled, cored, and
  diced
1 mango or papaya,
  peeled, deseeded,
  and diced
½–1 green chile, such as
  jalapeño or serrano,
  deseeded
  and chopped
½–1 red chile, such as
  jalapeño or serrano,
  chopped
½ red onion, chopped

1 tbsp sugar
juice of 1 lime
3 tbsp chopped fresh
  mint
salt

SCORCHED CHILE SALSA
1 green bell pepper
2–3 green chiles, such
  as jalapeño or
  serrano
2 garlic cloves, finely
  chopped
juice of ½ lime
1 tsp salt

large pinch of dried
  oregano
large pinch of ground
  cumin
2–3 tbsp extra-virgin
  olive oil or vegetable
  oil

SALSA VERDE
1 lb/450 g fresh
  tomatillos, husks
  removed, cooked in a
  small amount of
  water until just
  tender, then chopped

1–2 green chiles, such
  as jalapeño or
  serrano, deseeded
  and chopped finely
1 green bell pepper or
  large, mild green
  chile, such as
  Anaheim or poblano,
  deseeded and
  chopped
1 small onion, chopped
1 bunch fresh cilantro
  leaves, chopped finely
½ tsp ground cumin
salt

❶ To make Tropical Fruit Salsa, combine all the ingredients in a large bowl, adding salt to taste. Cover the bowl and chill in the refrigerator until required.

❷ To make Scorched Chile Salsa, char the chiles and bell pepper in an ungreased skillet. Cool, deseed, skin, and chop. Mix with the garlic, lime juice, salt, and oil. Top with oregano and cumin.

❸ To make Salsa Verde, combine the ingredients in a bowl, adding salt to taste. For a smoother sauce, blend the ingredients in a food processor. Spoon into a bowl to serve.

 very easy

 serves 4–6

 20 minutes

 15–20 minutes

Refried Bean Nachos

INGREDIENTS

14 oz/400 g refried
  beans
14 oz/400 g canned
  pinto beans, drained
large pinch of ground
  cumin
large pinch of mild chili
  powder
6 oz/175 g tortilla chips
2 cups grated cheese,
  such as Cheddar
salsa of your choice
1 avocado, pitted, diced,
  and tossed with lime
  juice
½ small onion or 3–5
  scallions, chopped
2 ripe tomatoes, diced
handful of shredded
  lettuce
3–4 tbsp chopped fresh
  cilantro
sour cream, to serve

❶ Place the refried beans in a pan with the pinto beans, cumin, and chili powder. Add enough water to make a thick, souplike consistency, stirring gently so the beans do not lose their texture.

❷ Heat the bean mixture over a medium heat until hot, then reduce the heat and keep warm while you prepare the rest of the dish.

❸ Put half the tortilla chips in the bottom of a flameproof casserole or gratin dish, and cover with the bean mixture. Sprinkle with the cheese and bake in a preheated oven at 400°F/200°C until the cheese melts. Alternatively, place the casserole under the broiler and broil for 5–7 minutes, or until the cheese melts and sizzles lightly in places.

❹ Arrange on top of the melted cheese the salsa, avocado, onion, tomato, lettuce, and fresh cilantro. Surround with the remaining tortilla chips and serve immediately, accompanied by sour cream.

 extremely easy

 serves 4

10 minutes

 20–25 minutes

Tortas

INGREDIENTS

4 crusty rolls, such as
French rolls or
bocadillos
melted butter or olive
oil, for brushing
1 cup refried beans
1½ cups each of
shredded cooked
chicken, browned
chorizo pieces, sliced
ham and cheese, or
any leftover cooked
meat you have to
hand
1 ripe tomato, sliced or
diced
1 small onion, chopped
finely
2 tbsp chopped fresh
cilantro
1 avocado, pitted,
sliced, and tossed
with lime juice
4–6 tbsp sour cream
salsa of your choice
handful of shredded
lettuce

❶ Cut the rolls in half and remove a little of the crumb to make space for the filling.

❷ Brush the outside and inside of the rolls with butter or oil, and toast, on both sides, on a hot griddle or in a skillet for a few minutes until crisp. Alternatively, place in a preheated oven at 400°F/200°C until toasted lightly.

❸ Meanwhile, place the beans in a pan with a very small amount of water and heat gently.

❹ When the rolls are heated, spread one half of each roll generously with the beans, then top with a layer of cooked meat. Top with tomato, onion, fresh cilantro, and avocado.

❺ Spread sour cream generously on the other side of each roll. Drizzle the salsa over the filling, add a little shredded lettuce, then sandwich the two sides of each roll together, pressing tightly. Serve immediately.

very easy

serves 4

10 minutes

5–10 minutes

Papaya, Avocado, & Red Bell Pepper Salad

INGREDIENTS

7 oz/200 g mixed green
    salad leaves
2–3 scallions, chopped
3–4 tbsp chopped fresh
    cilantro
1 small papaya
2 red bell peppers
1 avocado
1 tbsp lime juice
3–4 tbsp pumpkin
    seeds, preferably
    toasted (optional)

DRESSING
juice of 1 lime
large pinch of paprika,
large pinch of ground
    cumin
large pinch of sugar
1 garlic clove, chopped
    finely
4 tbsp extra-virgin olive
    oil
dash of white wine
    vinegar (optional)
salt

❶ Combine the salad leaves with the scallions and cilantro. Transfer to a serving dish.

❷ Cut the papaya in half and scoop out the seeds with a spoon. Cut into four, then remove the peel and slice the flesh. Arrange on top of the salad leaves. Cut the bell peppers in half and remove the cores and seeds, then slice thinly. Add to the salad leaves.

❸ Cut the avocado in half around the pit. Twist apart, then remove the pit with a knife. Peel off the skin carefully, dice the flesh, and toss in lime juice to prevent discoloration. Add to the other salad ingredients.

❹ To make the dressing, whisk together the lime juice, paprika, ground cumin, sugar, garlic, and olive oil. Add salt to taste.

❺ Pour the dressing over the salad and toss lightly, adding a dash of wine vinegar for a more intense flavor. Sprinkle with the toasted pumpkin seeds, if using, and serve the salad immediately.

 very easy

 serves 4

 15 minutes

 0 minutes

Green Bean Salad with Feta Cheese

12 oz/350 g green
  beans, trimmed
1 red onion, chopped
3–4 tbsp chopped fresh
  cilantro
2 radishes, sliced thinly
2³/₄ oz/75 g feta cheese,
  crumbled
1 tsp chopped fresh
  oregano or
  ¹/₂ tsp dried oregano
2 tbsp red wine or fruit
  vinegar
¹/₃ cup extra-virgin olive
  oil
3 ripe tomatoes, cut into
  wedges
pepper

1 Bring about 2 inches/5 cm water to a boil in the bottom of a steamer. Add the beans to the top part of the steamer, then cover, and steam for about 5 minutes, or until just tender.

2 Put the beans in a bowl and add the onion, cilantro, radishes, and feta cheese.

3 Sprinkle the oregano over the salad, then grind pepper on top to taste. Mix the vinegar and olive oil together and pour over the salad. Toss gently to mix well.

4 Transfer to a serving plate and surround with the tomato wedges. Serve at once, or chill until ready to serve.

 extremely easy

 serves 4

 10 minutes

 5 minutes

Mole Poblano

INGREDIENTS

3 fresh mulatto chiles
3 fresh mild ancho
  chiles
5–6 fresh Anaheim
  chiles
1 onion, chopped
5 garlic cloves, chopped
1 lb/450 g ripe tomatoes
2 tortillas, preferably
  stale, cut into small
  pieces
pinch of cloves
pinch of fennel seeds
1/8 tsp each ground
  cinnamon, coriander,
  and cumin
3 tbsp lightly toasted
  sesame seeds or
  tahini
3 tbsp slivered or
  coarsely ground
  blanched almonds
2 tbsp raisins
1 tbsp peanut butter
  (optional)
2 cups chicken bouillon
3–4 tbsp grated
  unsweetened
  chocolate
2 tbsp mild chili powder
3 tbsp vegetable oil
about 1 tbsp lime juice
salt and black pepper

❶ Using metal tongs, toast each chile over an open flame for a few seconds until the color darkens. Alternatively, roast in an ungreased skillet over a medium heat, turning constantly, for about 30 seconds.

❷ Place the toasted chiles in a bowl or a pan and cover them with boiling water. Cover with a lid and let soften for at least one hour, or preferably overnight. Once or twice, lift the lid and rearrange the chiles so that they soak evenly.

❸ Remove the softened chiles with a slotted spoon. Discard the stems and seeds, chop the flesh, and put it in a blender.

❹ Add the onion, garlic, tomatoes, tortillas, cloves, fennel seeds, cinnamon, coriander, cumin, sesame seeds, almonds, raisins, and peanut butter (if using), then process to combine. With the motor running, add enough bouillon through the feed tube to make a smooth paste. Stir in the remaining bouillon, chocolate, and chili powder.

❺ Heat the oil in a pan until it is smoking, then pour in the mole mixture. It will sputter and pop as it hits the oil. Cook for 10 minutes, stirring occasionally to prevent burning. Season with salt, pepper, and lime juice, and serve.

 easy

 serves 4

 10 minutes,
plus 1 hour
to soften

 15 minutes

Broccoli Enchiladas in Mild Chili Sauce

1 lb/450 g broccoli
    florets
8 oz/225 g ricotta
    cheese
1 garlic clove, chopped
½ tsp ground cumin
1½–2 cups Cheddar
    cheese, grated
6–8 tbsp freshly grated
    Parmesan cheese
1 egg, beaten lightly
4–6 flour tortillas
vegetable oil, for
    greasing
mild red chili sauce
1 cup chicken or
    vegetable bouillon
½ onion, chopped finely
3–4 tbsp chopped fresh
    cilantro
3 ripe tomatoes, diced
salt and pepper
hot salsa, to serve

❶ Bring a pan of salted water to a boil. Add the broccoli, then bring back to a boil and blanch for 1 minute. Drain, refresh under cold running water, then drain again. Cut off the broccoli stems, and peel and chop them. Dice the broccoli heads.

❷ Mix the broccoli with the ricotta cheese, garlic, cumin, half the Cheddar, and half the parmesan in a bowl. Mix in the egg, and season.

❸ Heat the tortillas in a lightly greased nonstick skillet, then fill each one with the broccoli mixture, and roll it up.

❹ Arrange the tortilla rolls in an ovenproof dish large enough to hold them in a single layer, then pour the mild chili sauce over the top. Pour the bouillon over the tortillas.

❺ Top with the remaining Cheddar and parmesan cheeses and bake in a preheated oven at 375°F/190°C for about 30 minutes. Serve sprinkled with the onion, fresh cilantro, and tomatoes. Serve with a hot salsa.

 very easy

 serves 4

 15 minutes

 40 minutes

Mexican Refried Beans "with everything"

INGREDIENTS

1–2 tbsp vegetable oil
1–1½ large onions,
    chopped
4½ oz/125 g bacon cut
    into small pieces
3–4 garlic cloves,
    chopped finely
about 1 tsp ground
    cumin
½ tsp mild chili powder
14 oz/400 g canned
    tomatoes, diced and
    drained, reserving
    about ²⁄₃–1 cup of
    their juices
14 oz/400 g refried beans,
    broken up into pieces
scant ½ cup beer
14 oz/400 g canned
    pinto beans, drained
salt and pepper

TO SERVE
warmed flour tortillas
sour cream
sliced pickled chilis

 very easy

 serves 4

 10 minutes

20 minutes

❶ Heat the oil in a skillet. Add the onion and bacon, and cook for about 5 minutes, or until they just turn brown. Stir in the garlic, cumin, and chili powder, and continue to cook for 1 minute. Add the tomatoes and cook over a medium–high heat until the liquid has evaporated.

❷ Add the refried beans and mash lightly in the pan with the tomato mixture, adding beer as needed to thin out the beans and make them smoother. Lower the heat and cook, stirring, until the mixture is smooth and creamy.

❸ Add the pinto beans and stir well to combine. If the mixture is too thick, add a little of the reserved tomato juice. Adjust the spicing to taste. Season with salt and pepper, and serve with warmed tortillas, sour cream, and sliced chilis.

 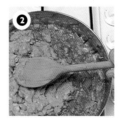 

COOK'S TIP
The length of time the beans take to cook will depend on their age – old beans take longer than younger beans.

Spicy, Fragrant Black Bean Chili

INGREDIENTS

14 oz/400 g dried black
    beans
2 tbsp olive oil
1 onion, chopped
5 garlic cloves, chopped
    coarsely
2 slices bacon, diced
$\frac{1}{2}$–1 tsp ground cumin
$\frac{1}{2}$–1 tsp mild red chili
    powder
1 red bell pepper, diced
1 carrot, diced
14 oz/400 g fresh toma-
    toes, diced, or
    chopped tomatoes,
    canned
1 bunch fresh cilantro,
    chopped coarsely
salt and pepper

 very easy

 serves 4

 10 minutes, plus
12 hours to soak

 2 hours, 45
minutes

❶ Soak the beans overnight, then drain. Put in a pan, then cover with water and bring to a boil. Boil for 10 minutes, reduce the heat, and simmer for about 1½ hours, or until tender. Drain well, reserving 1 cup of the cooking liquid.

❷ Heat the oil in a skillet. Add the onion and garlic and cook for 2 minutes, stirring, then add the bacon (if using), and cook, stirring occasionally, until the bacon is cooked and the onions are softened.

❸ Stir in the cumin and red chili powder and continue to cook for a moment or two. Add the red bell pepper, carrot, and tomatoes. Cook over a medium heat for 5 minutes.

❹ Add half the chopped fresh cilantro and the beans and their reserved liquid. Season with salt and pepper. Simmer for 30–45 minutes, or until the chili thickens and the flavor intensifies.

❺ Stir in the remaining cilantro, then adjust the seasoning and serve at once.

COOK'S TIP

If you use canned beans, instead of dried, drain and use 1 cup water for the liquid in Step 4.

Rice with Lime

INGREDIENTS

2 tbsp vegetable oil
1 small onion, chopped
 finely
3 garlic cloves, chopped
 finely
¾ cup mixed long-grain
 and wild rice
2 cups chicken or
 vegetable bouillon
juice of 1 lime
1 tbsp chopped fresh
 cilantro

❶ Heat the oil in a heavy-based pan or flameproof casserole. Add the onion and garlic and cook gently, stirring occasionally, for 2 minutes. Add the rice and cook for an additional minute, stirring. Pour in the bouillon, increase the heat and bring the rice to a boil. Reduce the heat to a very low simmer.

❷ Cover and cook the rice for about 10 minutes, or until the rice is just tender and the liquid is absorbed.

❸ Sprinkle in the lime juice and fork the rice to fluff up and to mix the juice in. Sprinkle with the cilantro and serve.

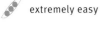 extremely easy

 serves 4

 5 minutes

 20 minutes

COOK'S TIP
Garnish the rice with sautéed plantains: slice a ripe peeled plantain on the diagonal, add a little oil to a heavy-based pan, and cook until the plantains have browned in spots and are tender. Arrange in the bowl of rice.

Eggs Oaxaca style

INGREDIENTS

2 lb 4 oz/1 kg ripe
    tomatoes
about 12 small pearl
    onions, halved
8 garlic cloves, whole
    and unpeeled
2 mild green chiles
pinch of ground cumin
pinch of dried oregano,
pinch of sugar, if
    needed
2–3 tsp vegetable oil
8 eggs, lightly beaten
1–2 tbsp tomato paste
salt and pepper
1–2 tbsp chopped fresh
    cilantro, to garnish

❶ Heat an ungreased skillet, then add the tomatoes and char lightly, turning them once or twice. Let cool.

❷ Meanwhile, char the onions, garlic, and chiles lightly in the skillet. Let cool slightly.

❸ Cut the cooled tomatoes into pieces and place in a blender or a food processor, with their charred skins. Remove the stems and seeds from the chiles, then peel and chop. Remove the skins from the garlic, and chop. Chop the onions coarsely. Add the chiles, garlic, and onions to the tomatoes.

❹ Process to make a rough purée, then add the cumin and oregano. Season with salt and pepper to taste, and add sugar if needed.

❺ Heat the oil in a heavy-based skillet, then add a ladleful of egg and cook to make a thin omelet. Continue to make omelets, stacking them on a plate as they cook. Slice them into ribbons.

❻ Bring the sauce to a boil, then adjust the seasoning, adding tomato paste to taste. Add the omelet strips and warm through, then serve at once, garnished with a sprinkling of fresh cilantro.

very easy

serves 4

15 minutes

25–30 minutes

Desserts

If your sizzling, spicy-hot Mexican meal has left your mouth on fire, the idea of a frozen dessert called Icy Fruit Blizzard will probably be very appealing, and this unusual dish is as cool and tastes as good as it sounds. Mexican Chocolate Meringues, served with strawberries, chocolate-flavored cream, and a sprinkling of cinnamon, round off a spicy dinner lightly and deliciously. The recipes in this part of the book are exotic compositions, with names to match. Aztec Oranges, for example, combines oranges with limes and Tequila, and empanadas are pastries with a filling of bananas and chocolate.

Aztec Oranges

INGREDIENTS

6 oranges
1 lime
2 tbsp Tequila
2 tbsp orange-flavored
    liqueur
dark soft brown sugar,
    to taste
fine lime zest strips, to
    decorate
    (see Cook's Tip)

❶ Using a sharp knife, cut a slice off the top and bottom of each of the oranges, then remove the peel and pith, cutting downward and taking care to retain the shape of the oranges.

❷ Holding each orange on its side, cut it horizontally into slices of even thickness.

❸ Place the oranges in a bowl. Cut the lime in half and squeeze over the oranges. Sprinkle with the Tequila and liqueur, then sprinkle sugar over the top.

❹ Chill until ready to serve, then transfer to a serving dish and garnish with lime strips.

 extremely easy

 serves 4

10 minutes,
plus 1 hour
to chill

0 minutes

COOK'S TIP
To make the decoration, pare the zest from a lime finely, using a vegetable peeler, then cut into thin strips. Add to boiling water and then blanch for 2 minutes. Drain in a strainer, and rinse under cold running water. Drain again and pat dry with paper towels.

Pineapple Compôte with Tequila & Mint

INGREDIENTS

1 ripe pineapple
sugar, to taste
juice of 1 lemon
2–3 tbsp Tequila or a
  few drops of vanilla
  extract
several sprigs of fresh
  mint, leaves removed,
  and cut into thin
  strips
fresh mint sprig, to
  decorate

❶ Using a sharp knife, cut off the top and bottom of the pineapple. Place upright on a board, then slice off the skin, cutting downward. Cut in half, remove the core if desired, then cut the flesh into slices and the slices into chunks.

❷ Put the pineapple in a bowl and sprinkle with the sugar, lemon juice, and Tequila or vanilla extract.

❸ Toss the pineapple to coat the chunks well, then chill until ready to serve.

❹ To serve, arrange on a serving plate and sprinkle with the mint strips. Decorate with a mint sprig.

extremely easy

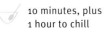
serves 4

10 minutes, plus
1 hour to chill

0 minutes

COOK'S TIP
Be careful to slice off the "eyes" when removing the skin from the pineapple.

Icy Fruit Blizzard

❶ Cover 2 baking sheets with a sheet of plastic wrap. Arrange the fruit on top and freeze for at least 2 hours, or until firm and icy.

❷ Place one type of fruit in a food processor and process until it is broken up into small pieces.

❸ Add a little orange juice and sugar, to taste, and continue to process until it forms a granular mixture. Repeat with the remaining fruit. Arrange in chilled bowls and serve immediately.

COOK'S TIP
All the fruit can be processed together, if preferred. Alternatively, use just one type of fruit and match the juice to the fruit.

Empanadas of Banana and Chocolate

INGREDIENTS

about 8 sheets of phyllo
    pastry, cut into half
    lengthwise
melted butter or
    vegetable oil, for
    brushing
2 ripe sweet bananas
1–2 tsp sugar
juice of ¼ lemon
6–7 oz/175–200 g
    semisweet chocolate,
    broken into small
    pieces
confectioner's sugar, for
    dusting
ground cinnamon, for
    dusting

 very easy

 serves 4

15 minutes

15 minutes

❶ Working one at a time, lay a long, rectangular sheet of phyllo in front of you and brush it with butter or oil.

❷ Peel and dice the bananas and place them in a bowl. Add the sugar and lemon juice, and stir well to combine. Stir in the chocolate.

❸ Place one or two teaspoons of the banana and chocolate mixture in one corner of the pastry, then fold over into a triangle shape to enclose the filling. Continue to fold in a triangular shape until all the phyllo is wrapped around the filling.

❹ Dust with confectioner's sugar and cinnamon. Place on a baking sheet and continue the process with the remaining phyllo pastry and filling.

❺ Bake in a preheated oven at 375°F/190°C for about 15 minutes, or until the little pastries are golden. Remove from the oven and serve hot, warning your guests that the filling is very hot.

COOK'S TIP
Use ready-made puff pastry instead of phyllo for a more fluffy effect.

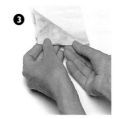

Torta del Cielo

1 Butter an 8 inch/20 cm round or square cake pan lightly and line it with baking parchment.

2 Put the almonds in a food processor to form a crumbly mixture. Set aside.

3 Beat the butter and sugar in a bowl until they form a smooth, fluffy mixture. Beat in the eggs, almonds, and the almond and vanilla extracts until well blended.

4 Stir in the flour and salt, and mix briefly, until the flour is just incorporated.

5 Pour or spoon the batter into the greased pan and smooth the surface. Bake in a preheated oven at 350°F/180°C for 40–50 minutes, or until the cake feels spongy when gently pressed.

6 Remove from the oven, and let cool on a wire rack. To serve, dust with confectioner's sugar and decorate with toasted almonds.

very easy

serves 4

15 minutes

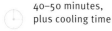
40–50 minutes,
plus cooling time

Mexican Chocolate Meringues

 very easy

serves 4

10 minutes

3 hours

❶ Whisk the egg whites until they are foamy, then add the salt and cream of tartar and beat until very stiff. Whisk in the vanilla, then slowly whisk in the sugar, a small amount at a time, until the meringue is shiny and stiff. This should take about 3 minutes by hand, and under a minute with an electric beater.

❷ Whisk in the cinnamon and grated chocolate. Spoon mounds, about 2 tablespoonfuls, on to an ungreased nonstick baking sheet. Space the mounds well.

❸ Place in a preheated oven at 300° F/150° C and cook for 3 hours, or until set.

❹ Carefully remove from the baking sheet. If the meringues are too moist and soft, return them to the oven to firm up and dry out more. Let cool completely.

❺ Serve the meringues dusted with cinnamon and accompanied by strawberries and chocolate-flavored cream.

COOK'S TIP

To make the flavored cream, simply stir half-melted chocolate pieces into stiffly whipped cream, then chill until solid.